TADPOLE STORY

Angela Royston

Crabtree Publishing Company

www.crabtreebooks.com

2/12
21 27

Author: Angela Royston
Editors: Kathy Middleton
       Crystal Sikkens
Project coordinator: Kathy Middleton
Production coordinator: Ken Wright
Prepress technicians: Ken Wright
       Margaret Amy Salter

Picture Credits:
Corbis: Jean Hall/Cordaiy Photo Library Ltd: page 7;
  Naturfoto Honal: page 10
Dreamstime: Christian Bernfeld: page 17; Dirk Ercken:
  pages 3, 20; Ou Fei: page 9; Gedewe: page 4; George
  Hopkins: page 19; Jubalharshaw19: page 15; Maxim
  Petrichuk: page 21; Szefei: page 5; Zarozinia: page 18
Photolibrary: Rosemary Calvert: page 8; Reinhard Hölzl:
  page 6
Shutterstock: cover; Tony Campbell: page 13; Matt Hart:
  page 16; Payless Images: page 12; Snowlena: page 14;
  Wolfgang Staib: pages 1, 11

Library and Archives Canada Cataloguing in Publication

Royston, Angela
    Tadpole story / Angela Royston.

(Crabtree connections)
Includes index.
ISBN 978-0-7787-7859-2 (bound).--ISBN 978-0-7787-7881-3 (pbk.).

    1. Frogs--Life cycles--Juvenile literature. 2. Tadpoles--Juvenile
literature. I. Title. II. Series: Crabtree connections

QL668.E2R69 2011   j597.8'9139   C2011-900598-0

Library of Congress Cataloging-in-Publication Data

Royston, Angela, 1945-
    Tadpole story / Angela Royston.
      p. cm. -- (Crabtree connections)
  Includes index.
  ISBN 978-0-7787-7881-3 (pbk. : alk. paper) -- ISBN 978-0-7787-7859-2
(reinforced library binding : alk. paper)
  1. Tadpoles--Juvenile literature. I. Title.
  QL668.E2R658 2012
  597.8'139--dc22
                  2011001331

Crabtree Publishing Company

www.crabtreebooks.com   1-800-387-7650

Printed in the U.S.A./072011/WO20110114

Published in Canada
Crabtree Publishing
616 Welland Ave.
St. Catharines, Ontario
L2M 5V6

Published in the United States
Crabtree Publishing
PMB 59051
350 Fifth Avenue, 59th Floor
New York, New York 10118

Contents

My World 4

Starting Out 6

Out of the Egg 8

No More Gills 10

A Lot of Food 12

Look—Two Legs 14

Four Legs 16

A Froglet 18

Living on Land 20

Glossary 22

Further Reading 23

Index 24

My World

I am a **tadpole**, and I live in a pond. One day soon I will change from a tiny tadpole into a fully grown frog. Then I will hop out onto the land!

See me change

I am changing all the time. Read my story and see what happens to me as I grow from a tiny speck into a frog.

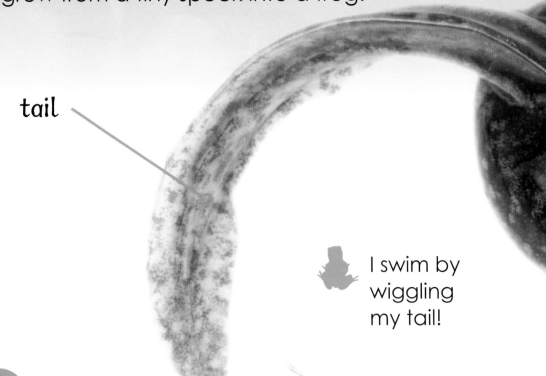

tail

I swim by wiggling my tail!

Just like mom

One day I will turn into a frog, just like my mom and dad. Will I look like this?

Starting Out

I began my life as a black dot in a lump of jelly! The jelly is called **frogspawn**, and it floated on the surface of the pond.

Bye, Mom!
My mom **laid** the frogspawn then swam away. I never saw her again. Fish eat frogspawn, but luckily they didn't eat me!

Each black dot in this frogspawn is a tiny tadpole.

tadpole

Sticky eggs

Each tadpole grows
inside its own egg.
Sticky jelly holds
the eggs together.

Out of the Egg

I grew in the frogspawn for two weeks, then I was ready to **hatch**. I wriggled out of my egg and clung onto the jelly.

Getting stronger

I ate the jelly and grew stronger and stronger, until I was strong enough to swim away. I had **gills** on the sides of my head.

Not alone

My brothers and sisters hatched out, too, so the pond was full of tadpoles.

I used my gills to breathe underwater.

gill

9

No More Gills

My gills did not last long.
After just ten days, my gills
closed up. I began to grow
lungs inside my body instead.

Up to the surface

Sometimes I swam up to the surface to
eat tiny plants that floated on the water.
I didn't swim to the surface to breathe
in air until my lungs were fully grown.

Eat, eat, eat

Tadpoles love to eat! We swam around the pond looking for tiny plants to eat.

Look—no more gills!

A Lot of Food

The more I ate, the bigger I grew. My body became so fat and round that many animals wanted to eat me! It was a dangerous time.

Nearly caught

One day I was nearly caught by a fish, but I twisted and turned and managed to swim away. Phew!

 My strong tail helped me swim.

Danger!

The pond is a dangerous place. Every animal is lunch for something else.

Look—Two Legs

When I was five weeks old, my back legs began to grow. At first they were very small and weak, but they quickly grew bigger and stronger.

Swimming with legs

When I swam, I used my legs as well as my tail. I grew skin between my toes so I could push against the water.

leg

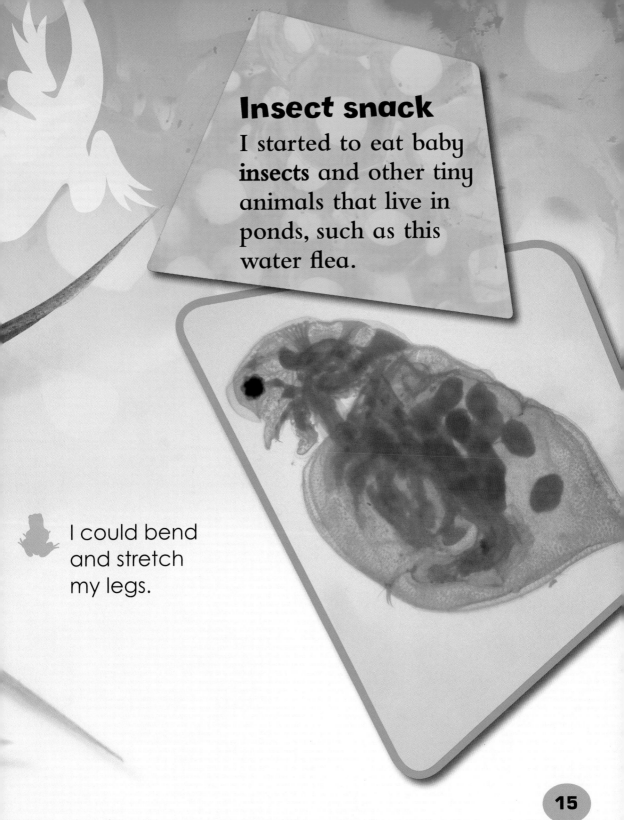

Insect snack

I started to eat baby **insects** and other tiny animals that live in ponds, such as this water flea.

I could bend and stretch my legs.

Four Legs

When I was about eight weeks old, two small bumps began to grow on the outside of my body where my gill slits used to be.

Nearly there

The bumps changed into two more legs. Now I had four legs, but I still had my tail. I was halfway between a tadpole and a frog. What happened next?

My skin was brown and speckled.

front leg

Not me!

This **newt** tadpole
lives in the pond. Its
front legs grew before
its back legs.

A Froglet

By the time I was just 12 weeks old, I had changed into a tiny frog. I had come a long way since I was in the frogspawn.

First jumps

One day I climbed out of the pond and sat on a floating leaf. Then I took my very first jump on dry land!

 Look how short my tail had become!

Teeny weeny

This frog is no bigger than your fingernail! It can fit inside a flower.

tail

Living on Land

Now I am one year old. I spend most of my time on land, but I never go far from water. I jump in to keep my skin wet.

Hide and seek

It's hard to see me in the water, but I can see really well! When a fly comes by, I catch it with my long, sticky tongue.

eye

My eyes are on top of my head.

Slithery snake

On land, I watch out for snakes and other animals that might want to eat me.

Glossary

frogspawn A lot of frog eggs stuck together with jelly

gills Parts of the body that are used to breathe in water. Tadpoles, fish, and many other water animals have gills.

hatch When an animal or insect breaks out of its egg

laid Made eggs and deposited them

lungs Parts of the body used to breathe in air

insects Small animals with six legs and often two wings. Flies, butterflies, and ladybugs are all insects.

newt Small animal that lives some of its life in water and some of it on land

slits Long narrow openings

tadpole Young frog before it has grown legs

Further Reading

Web Sites

Find out how to tell frogs from toads at:
www.42explore.com/frogs.htm

You can find a lot of information about tadpoles and frogs, as well as fun things to do, at:
www.allaboutfrogs.org

This site has a lot of facts about frogs, with activities and worksheets, too. You can find it at:
www.enchantedlearning.com/subjects/amphibians/frogs

Books

Tadpoles to Frogs by Bobbie Kalman, Crabtree Publishing (2009).

Metamorphosis: Changing Bodies by Bobbie Kalman and Kathryn Smithyman, Crabtree Publishing Company (2005).

Life in a Pond by Adam Hibbert and Jolyon Goddard, Gareth Stevens Learning Library (2010).

Index

breathing 9, 10

eating 8, 10–11, 12, 15, 20
eggs 7, 8
eyes 20

fish 6, 12
fly 20
frog 4, 5, 6, 18–19, 20–21
froglet 18–19
frogspawn 6–7, 8, 18

gills 8, 9, 10, 11, 16

hatch 8–9

insects 15

jelly 6, 7, 8
jump 18, 20, 21

legs 14, 15, 16–17
lungs 10

newt 17

plants 10–11

skin 14, 16, 20
snakes 21

tail 4, 12, 14, 16, 18, 19